Praises for

Marriage

I heartily recommend this quick read book on the basics of 'tying the knot' to any couple, or single person, seeking God's Will for their life in regard to the second-most important decision and step in their life – that of marriage. Dr. Keith lays out in an easy-to-read, practical, format, common-sense insight, fortified thoroughly with Biblical admonition. It's a 'well worth it' read for anyone thinking about marriage, as well as for those already married. Read it, and be instructed, challenged, and strengthened.

—Martin J. Shott
Senior Pastor of Harvest Baptist Church
New Hartford, CT

***

This book presents itself as a conversation about marriage; one of the most sacred and important relationships to mankind. Keith is extremely transparent, personal about his own experiences, and inspirational in his thoughts about this life-long commitment. Keith's usage of the Scriptures throughout this book lends the foundational support needed for the reader when navigating through his marital and pre-marital journey. From cover to cover, this book will provide a fresh reminder of marriage for every person seeking to honor God and to prepare himself for this wonderful union called marriage.

—Dan Shafer
Lead Pastor
All Nations Baptist Church
www.allnationsbaptist.org

***

Dr. Pelletier's writing is relevant and applicable, filled with life-tested and scripture-informed encouragement on marriage and relationships. It is a worthwhile read that covers pre-marital and post-marital phases; therefore, a helpful navigational aid for a broad audience of people looking to gain awareness and enhance their relationships. Readers will gain valuable tools and a greater understanding of identifying, managing, and conquering obstacles in life. You will enjoy the read and find it filled with practicality and honesty, a great opportunity to learn and grow.

—Dr. Sara Longan
Instructional Mentor and Assistant Professor
Liberty University

***

The author brings important common sense issues in the matter of dating and marriage to the forefront in a transparent and enjoyable way. Whether you are hoping to be married in the future or are presently married you will find helpful information here for building a successful and Christ-centered relationship.

—Tony Bulawa
Far North Director
Baptist International Missions, Inc.

***

Dr. Pelletier's book is an invaluable resource for couples in all stages. Finding a life partner can be tricky. Having a healthy relationship is even more complex at times. This book provides genuine and relevant advice for creating healthy relationships. ***Doing the I Do in Marriage*** is a must-read book for those searching for their life partner and those who are married.

—Dr. Jeffry Caballero
President of Harbor Genesis Christian College & Board Member of the Association for Hispanic Theological Education (AETH)

Marriage

Doing the I Do in Marriage

By Keith J. Pelletier, PhD, MBA, MHS, CCP

Published by KHARIS PUBLISHING, imprint of KHARIS MEDIA LLC.

Copyright © 2021 Keith J. Pelletier

ISBN-13: 978-1-63746-081-8

ISBN-10: 1-63746-081-3

Library of Congress Control Number: 2021950034

All rights reserved. This book or parts thereof may not be reproduced in any form, stored in a retrieval system, or transmitted in any form by any means - electronic, mechanical, photocopy, recording, or otherwise - without prior written permission of the publisher, except as provided by United States of America copyright law.

All Scripture quotations, unless otherwise indicated, are taken from the Holy Bible, KING JAMES VERSION (KJV): KING JAMES VERSION, public domain.

All KHARIS PUBLISHING products are available at special quantity discounts for bulk purchase for sales promotions, premiums, fundraising, and educational needs. For details, contact:

Kharis Media LLC
Tel: 1-479-599-8657
support@kharispublishing.com
www.kharispublishing.com

Table of Contents

1	Introduction	1
2	Knowing What You Want	5
3	Looking for What You Want	26
4	Finding What You Want	38
5	Tying the Knot	57
6	Navigating a Lot	69
7	Keeping What You Got	79
8	Conclusion	86
	Acknowledgment	89

1 Introduction

My name is Keith Pelletier and my wife is Kristen Pelletier. We have been married since 09/10/11. We have read our share of marriage and couples books that focused on a healthy relationship, but, honestly, the best book that is out there for this topic (and we really do suggest you buy it) is the Bible.

The Bible has been available for everyone ever since its author, God, wrote it about 4,000 years ago. The Bible is the best reference guide you can use for any topic, and we wanted to offer a book that could offer specific guidance while also referencing the Bible.

In this book, I discuss the topic of marriage. I really do love talking about marriage, and specifically our marriage. We were not high school sweethearts, but we did go to the same high school. We were not in the same grade, I am three years older than Kristen, and she only went to that high school for her senior year. We knew of each other but did not really know each other back then.

It was not until we had both finished our undergraduate degrees that we reconnected and started dating. We dated for just under a year, and we were engaged for just under a year before we got married. I was 28, and Kristen was 25 when we made our promise to each other and to God that we would be married until death do us part.

And that is exactly what a marriage is, a holy covenant that is made to always be with each other for all time. It is not just an extension of dating, when people can part ways whenever it gets rough. There will be difficult times throughout your marriage, but we hope this book can help you navigate through any problems so you can enjoy your marriage like you probably did on your wedding day.

Let me be clear though.

My best advice will be pointing you to the Bible. If you bought this book thinking that you would have a guarantee that you would never struggle in your marriage ever again, then you will be disappointed. If you bought this book thinking I lived a perfect example of how a marriage should be, you would be wrong again.

I can only give information regarding what you should do for a successful marriage, but everyone makes mistakes.

Romans 3:23: "***For all have sinned, and come short of the glory of God;***"

Nobody in life is perfect; and unfortunately, that means your marriage will not always be perfect.

To be honest, I definitely have my faults in life. I am probably like most men and have to be careful with my eyes. I am not going to pretend to be better than I am or better than anyone else.

Proverbs 27:20: "***Hell and destruction are never full; so the eyes of man are never satisfied.***"

My wife is also not perfect; she needs to be careful to be content with everything and not think about what life could be like under different circumstances.

Exodus 20:17: "***Thou shalt not covet thy neighbour's house, thou shalt not covet thy neighbour's wife, nor***

Introduction

his manservant, nor his maidservant, nor his ox, nor his ass, nor any thing that is thy neighbour's."

But this is why you need to constantly do the doing in marriage that will sustain the love and keep your marriage successful.

Your marriage will not always be rainbows and butterflies, but it also will not always be doom and gloom either. You will go through different seasons and times throughout your life. And you need to support each other so that you can be victorious in each situation.

Ecclesiastes 3:4,8: "***⁴A time to weep, and a time to laugh; a time to mourn, and a time to dance; ⁸A time to love, and a time to hate; a time of war, and a time of peace.***"

Even though we might go through hard times, God is the source of our victory.

I Corinthians 15:57: "***But thanks be to God, which giveth us the victory through our Lord Jesus Christ.***"

The important thing is what you do or how you react after those imperfect times. And that is the purpose of this book to try to show you how to deal with the reality involved with marriage.

I look at a few areas pertaining to before and during marriage that are important in supporting a healthy and happy marriage. We use some of our personal experiences to share just how vital these areas are. The topics we discuss are:

- knowing what you want,

- looking for what you want,
- finding what you want,
- tying the knot,
- navigating a lot, and
- keeping what you got

Before I get into the details, I want to point out that when you get married, you verbally agree to the marriage by saying, "I do." This is a present tense action verb.

You don't say "I did" or "I will." This mean that you will continually be *doing* throughout your marriage, continually *doing*, to make sure that it is a happy and healthy marriage.

You'll read in James 1:22: "***But be ye doers of the word, and not hearers only, deceiving your own selves.***"

Hearing the words, "I do" is sweet and romantic. If you only hear those words, but there is no doing that backs up those words, you will be deceiving yourself and your spouse.

So, as you read this book, please remember that being married is something you have to do, not something that just happens to you.

2   Knowing What You Want

So simple, right? You just have to know what you want. And since you know yourself, you should already know everything that you could ever want. But there is a problem with this thought.

We are talking about things that you WANT. Did you ever, in your entire existence, change your mind about something that you wanted?

I hope you didn't just say "no" in your head.

If you are anything like me and my wife, you change your minds --just like we change ours -- as often as gas prices change.

We can be ordering food in the drive-thru and change our minds three different times before finalizing the order. As we drive up to the window to pick up our order, we ask each other why the other person ordered what they did.

My wife will say to me, "I thought you weren't going to eat donuts anymore?"

As soon as I take my first bite of the donut, I immediately wish I hadn't done that. And so many times, my wife will complain that her coffee doesn't taste good, or they must have messed up something in making her coffee.

But marriage is a life-long commitment. You should not be changing your mind after you get married, so you better make sure you know what you want before you get married.

Read Mark 10:7-9: *"For this cause shall a man leave his father and mother, and cleave to his wife; ⁸And they twain shall be one flesh: so then they are no more twain, but one flesh. ⁹What therefore God hath joined together, let not man put asunder."*

First, this verse about your marriage states you are no longer two different people but you are now one flesh. You will need to face things together and support one another in all things.

Once you are married, no one should separate the two of you. This was spoken by Jesus Christ himself, so you know that marriage really should last forever. Since it is a forever choice, maybe you should look a little further into your thinking about your marriage and make sure that you know what you want.

What kind of things should you take into consideration? Well, since this is a forever decision, you should take into consideration... EVERYTHING.

Since I couldn't list every single situation or criteria in this book, I covered some of the more important ones.

Religion

I guess this is the best place to start. My wife and I are both Christians, and I am using the Bible throughout this book, so it is only natural that I first talk about how much of an impact religion makes on people's lives. Religion is what you believe in, and it is a way of life.

Since I am writing on these topics in these pages, you will probably wonder where my wife and I are in regards to each area. Regarding religion, I grew up in a Christian family since I was born. My parents grew up Catholic, and they were each the first people in their family to get saved. My wife grew up in a Christian family as well, and her dad has been a Baptist pastor of the same church in Connecticut since 1985.

If your religion is what compels you to live your life the way you do, and it influences the decisions you make, then it does all the same stuff for your spouse, too. How easy do you think the rest of your life would be if you believe in different things than your spouse?

Take a look at II Corinthians 6:14: **"Be ye not unequally yoked together with unbelievers: for what fellowship hath righteousness with unrighteousness? And what communion hath light with darkness?"**

This passage is speaking about the warning of born-again believers in Christ being married to non-believers. Does this happen? Yes. Does this happen often? Of course.

However, we have been friends with many couples where there is both a believer and a non-believer; they could tell you themselves how difficult that is for their entire household. It is not just a matter of whether you pray for your food or not, it is your entire life. Your religion is what sets the foundation of your life and everything that you do.

Let's say that someone in the relationship is saved, but the other person is not. When they are dating, or maybe early in their relationship, the unsaved person will go to church with the believer. They might do this because they just naturally like the believer and would do "anything" for them at this time, but then there can be a time when the unbeliever decides they do not need to put on that act anymore.

Now, there are two different paths that this example can take: One, the unsaved person will stop going to church, resentment will occur in the relationship, and more hardship will have to be endured. The second path is that after tirelessly witnessing and being a testimony, the unsaved person will really have a desire to hear more and eventually come to know the Lord as their personal Savior.

Either can happen, depending on how much you pray for their salvation. However, there will be some bumps in the road down this path. II Corinthians 6:14 talks about how righteousness and unrighteousness do not have a good relationship. The saved person will want to serve the Lord, while the unsaved person will want to satisfy the desire of their flesh.

But read in Romans 8:8: "**So then they that are in the flesh cannot please God.**"

This will not only affect the husband and the wife in the relationship, but it will also affect the children, the extended family, and others that are close to this couple.

The children will grow up looking at their parents' example, with both mom and dad on different pages in their marriage. The saved person can do whatever they want to show their children how to serve God, but the devil also has a good opportunity in distracting the children from serving God.

The parent who allows their children stay home playing video games, or anything else they want, might seem more appealing for the children than waking up early, dressing up, and sitting still in church.

This subject does not just apply to those individuals who want to stay home sleeping in instead of going to church. This topic is important for people with different religions as well. If the mom believes in one thing, and the dad believes something else, this will also create a very confusing foundation for their children.

Religion does not simply mean what you believe, but it is how you live your life.

Age

Age. This is a difficult topic, but it does need to be considered when trying to find out what you want in a marriage. Ultimately, this topic will be entirely up to the individuals in the relationship, but there are a few things to think about before ignoring age entirely, and referring to it as "just a number."

Now, before I go any further, I do want to say that I have seen all extreme situations with people's ages in marriage. We know couples where the wife is about 20 years older than the husband. We know couples where the husband is about 20 years older than the wife.

When I was a teenager, I went to church with this older couple in which the husband and wife had the exact same birth date, month, and year. This couple even had the same name, with only slightly different spellings in their first names. I mean, this definitely seems like a cute story, but it also can cause its own awkward situations.

That said, there is no exact number or formula you need to follow to make sure you find a soulmate that is a "correct" age. There are some ground rules that can apply when considering this topic.

You want to have some things in common with the person with whom you will spend the rest of your life. Does this mean that you have to be born in the same year or within 24 months of each other? That is not for us to say. The real desire is to have common ground together.

The more of an age gap between the couple means that they grew up in different times. They have fewer things to relate to, whether it is music, tv shows, style, culture, events, etc. You might not always and only talk about the best shows from the '90s in conversation, and your spouse talk always and only about the "Golden Age" of tv, but the cultural and circumstantial experiences can shift how people think and react to certain things.

If you are closer to, or at least at a relatable age, you will be going through the same life events at similar times. When you are still young, you both might want to travel or to vacation at places that interest both of you. Couples with similar ages will have to go through retirement together. If there is a very large age gap, one person will be retiring while the other person will still have to go to work every day.

By itself, this will not end a relationship, but when you start to think about how the body starts to fail in older age, it can put stress on a relationship. If there is a 20 year age gap, people in their 40s or 50s will probably still be very active, but their spouses would be in their 60s or 70s, and they might not be able to get around as easily.

If the older spouse dies in their old age, their younger spouse might have to spend their next 20 years alone in their old age if they are healthy. This can be a very lonely time in their lives, especially if they do not have much family to visit them.

Depending on age, one person might not be able to have children, while the other person might want children. One spouse might be young enough to keep up with the high energy of children, while the other spouse is not able to keep up with the children.

I am 3 years older than my wife. For us, this is a good age gap for us. Three years is definitely not the magic number in every marriage though. You actually do not have to stress too much about it right away. This will be something that you can feel for as you date someone. If you start to realize you do not relate with someone as you are dating, maybe age is playing a significant role for you.

Height

Here is a good topic that I definitely wanted to include in this book. My wife is 5 foot 2 inches, and I identify as 6 feet tall. (My wife made sure that I put in here that I am actually *not* 6 feet tall. I am 5 foot 6 inches.) I am taller than my wife, but depending on the size heels that my wife wears, I can easily become less tall than her.

Does height even make a difference in your relationship? I am still asked to reach for things on the top shelf, but I purposely put things on the top shelf just so I can feel special for being the only one of us who can reach it. However, we do have our share of step stools throughout our house. Right now we are able to use the excuse that we have those step stools so that "our kids can reach things." Yes, that is the reason.

So, is height important? It is if it is important to you.

There is nothing written down where it says the husband must be taller than the wife. This should just be in accordance to your comfort level. Do you want to be the same height, taller, or shorter than your spouse?

For me, I wanted to be taller than the person I married. Not everyone even has to worry too much about this topic. But on the opposite end of the spectrum, if the guy is 6 foot 8 inches, and the girl is 5 foot nothing, they will have other struggles in life, like getting cramps in their necks when they try to kiss each other.

Take I Samuel 16:7 into consideration: "***But the LORD said unto Samuel, Look not on his countenance, or on the height of his stature; because I have refused him: for the LORD seeth not as man seeth; for man looketh on the outward appearance, but the LORD looketh on the heart.***"

As long as you and your spouse are happy with each other's height, you will be all set, but you will first need to determine what it is that you want.

Location

"Location, location, location." Location has long been a critical factor in finding a spouse, however, with the use of the internet, social media, and various dating websites, location has dropped a notch in importance.

Obviously, you will meet new people in the traditional in-person fashion more than you likely will in the digital fashion.

The ability to meet someone in-person gives more weight to the criteria that you already have something in common with that person. Finding common interests is one of the first things people look for when looking for their spouse.

If you realize that the same person is in some of your classes in college, you might have a good common background to share. You might be pursuing similar degrees, or you might simply have similar interests in that field of study. Regardless, schoolmates are a common source of finding a spouse.

I do not need to make a list of places where you might meet someone because there are endless possibilities. What you do need to consider is if you meet someone while on vacation and they live thousands of miles away from you, it would take a great deal of effort to make that relationship successful.

Can it work? Yes. But you would have to figure out which person would move closer to the other person's home, or both of you would have to move to a different location where you would be able to actually visit each other.

Sometimes people prefer to live in the same area their entire lives, and for these people, they would benefit more with someone living closer to them. Other people have no anchors in their lives. They are just looking for a reason to make their next move and these people would not struggle that much with someone who lives farther away.

I do know a couple where the husband works in one state, and his wife lives hundreds of miles away from where he works. This man works contract jobs, and when he has a contract location that is a few hour drive; he would drive to visit his wife on the weekends that he did not have to work. When he worked further than a few hour drive, he would not get to see his wife for about 13 weeks at a time. He was doing this for many years when I knew him, and supposedly this worked for him. However, I would not suggest this situation for anyone.

Considering longer distance relationships, our culture does foster the formation of these relationships with social media and dating websites. These tools allow people to "meet" when they would never typically meet each other in person. This can have its benefits of sifting through some options by reading about their interests and without wasting much time. Some drawbacks are that some interactions can be awkward when not in person, and some of these virtual options cost money to use.

These digital tools have become much more frequently used lately, and many people do not think twice about meeting other people this way.

My wife and I basically met this way. We did go to the same high school, but I was 3 grades ahead of her, so we did not really know each other. She was in the same class as one of my very close family friends, so we heard each other's names and a little about each other. It was not until we both finished our undergraduate degrees that we decided to reconnect and get to know each other.

Also, do not forget Genesis 13:12-13: "***Abram dwelled in the land of Canaan, and Lot dwelled in the cities of the plain, and pitched his tent toward Sodom. ¹³But the men of Sodom were wicked and sinners before the LORD exceedingly.***"

Pick a location that will help you in serving the Lord. Do not pick a place that will just set you up for failure in your marriage. Do not be like Lot, who chose to live right next to great sin, temptation, and wickedness.

Job

Having a job is unavoidable; you need to have some kind of job to earn money so that you can survive in this world. Speaking of which, this world is very expensive. I am seeing many more people waiting until they are older to get married because they do not have enough money saved up for a house, family, or a wedding. Unless you are an heir or heiress to a billion-dollar corporation, you will need to go out and apply for a job one day soon enough.

I am not only talking to teenagers here; I know many adults who are still trying to figure out what their next job will be so that they can live more comfortably.

It is difficult enough to determine what job you will want for your life, but it is even more difficult when you take into consideration how a job can affect a marriage.

If you have a job in which you are constantly travelling, it limits you to certain people who would want to share that lifestyle. Sure, travelling and seeing the world can sound like a fun adventure, but not everyone wants to entirely uproot their lives every so often. Maybe your job takes you away only a few days or couple weeks at a time, or maybe you are in the military and you will be moving across the country with your family or getting deployed without your family.

It all depends on your desire and commitment level. You have to be careful about location because you will need to have some good quality time with your spouse so that you can build and flourish in your marriage.

A typical job requires a person to work about 8 hours a day, at least. Now consider that we are told we need about 8 hours a day to support a healthy functioning body. Time to do math: there are only 24 hours in a day, so you are also spending about 8 hours with your spouse while you are awake.

Maybe you stay awake longer with your spouse, but now you are losing the sleep you need. What if you work longer than 8 hours a day at your job, like many people do; now you have even less than 8 hours with your spouse each day.

At the very worst, you spend the same amount of time at work as you do interacting with your spouse. This shows that you need to have a job that you will enjoy, and a job that will not interfere with your marriage.

I know people who work opposite shifts to their spouse's. The one person would work first shift, and the other would work third shift. This recipe leads to having much less time together than working the same shift as each other. Of course, sometimes things are unavoidable. For this example, the couple did this because it helped them with their child; they did not have anyone to watch their child if they both worked the same shift.

What about the opposite end of the spectrum? What if the couple worked at the same job? At first, this would be pretty great. But then you might have to realize that work gets stressful at times. Working together can cause some of that stress to be shared with, or even worse, towards each other.

Working together can make it easier to share your daily activities together when you are trying to vent or decompress from the stress of work. However, it might create the environment where both of you are tired about hearing about work, and now neither of you can help support one another when you need to vent.

This is one reason why I have met so many people who have made it a rule not to date anyone with whom they work.

For my wife and me, my wife currently stays home with our young children, but in our case, I work in the medical field and am often required to be on call. I work with heart surgery, and I am the person who stops the heart and takes over the functions of the heart and lungs during surgery.

With this type of job, I often get called in for emergency surgery. We are married with four young children, so obviously, this is not the greatest scenario for us. I started going to school for this profession before I started dating my wife; I was single and did not mind the endless hours that I had to work.

In the first job I had in this profession when we were married, I was working much more than 60 hours a week. There were times when I would not come home for a couple days, or I was called back into work as soon as I pulled into our driveway.

This was part of my job, and I do enjoy this work and saving lives, but I also knew that it was very difficult for my wife to be home non-stop with our children without any breaks. We were finally fortunate enough when I was able to transfer my job to another hospital that was far less busy, and I did not get called in as much. We finally achieved a much better quality of life and work-life balance.

It is important to have a job that can help support your marriage; it is also very important that you make adjustments to your job to promote a healthier marriage. Marriage and jobs are both important. While you will retire from your job one day, you should not retire from your spouse.

See Ecclesiastes 9:10: "***Whatsoever thy hand findeth to do, do it with thy might; for there is no work, nor device, nor knowledge, nor wisdom, in the grave, whither thou goest***."

Make sure you are a hard worker that also works hard for your family.

Like I said earlier, I work in heart surgery. So please believe me when I tell you about how important it is to take good care of your heart, physically and emotionally.

The food that you put in your life will affect your physical heart, but the actions and events in your life will affect your emotional heart.

What do you think would happened to the patient's heart if I didn't do my best to care for the heart. The patient could get injured or even die. I need to pay attention constantly to what is happening to the heart.

What do you think would happen to your hearts if you do not do your best to care for your spouse? Your marriage could get hurt or even end in a divorce. You need to pay attention constantly to what is happening to each other's heart.

Kids

Here is the topic I would have thought people actually talked about before getting married, but so many times I see that is not the case. I have known so many people who found each other, fell in love, and got married, but then only months later, they got a divorce because they could not agree on having children or not.

For my wife and me, we had an entire list of names (first and middle names) for all of our future children before we even got engaged. It is something that we both talked about often, to make sure we had the same desires for a family. Marriage is a commitment and promise for your entire life, so you might as well talk about every topic, especially the one that makes each spouse a parent.

Now, picking names might be a little bit overboard and unnecessary, as long as we are in agreeance with children. Now we also know people who are the other extreme with children. Some couples agree that they want children, but they sometimes do not name their children until the kids were a few days old; Some couples ask advice for names, pick names randomly, or name the children after someone close to them. I am sure that the names all turn out to be good names, but at least they had the conversation about both of them wanting children before they were married.

It can be as simple as, "Do you want to have kids one day?" But it would be a good idea to also ask about timelines. Some people might want to start having children the second they get married, but other people might want to relax, travel, or get to know each other for a few years before having children. Age might play a factor in this, but it can also be personal preference. The only way to know is to find out. The only way to find out is to talk about it.

We wanted to have our children soon after we got married. We were not necessarily old when we got married, but we were not very young either. We did not want to wait until we were older to have kids. We wanted to be young enough to have the energy to keep up with our kids.

Oh, that is the other part of the subject: How many kids?

Remember, you do not have to set anything in stone about how many kids both of you want, but it is good to have an idea. Do you want only one? Only two? An even number of kids? An odd number of kids? As many as possible? Let's see what happens? etc.

So many things can play a role in, and can change your preference, for how many children you want. Maybe there was a very difficult pregnancy, and you do not want to go through that again. Maybe the child was born with a medical condition that made you too scared or unsure about having more children. Maybe you realize it is too much work being too outnumbered with children.

My wife and I wanted a good-sized family. We both wanted at least four children, and we had four children. My wife did have a couple difficult pregnancies that made us not want to get pregnant again, but we both wanted more children. As I wrote this, we were in the middle of trying to adopt children.

That is the other side of this topic. Do you want children naturally? IVF? Foster? Adopt? There are reasons for each choice, and the choice is up to you, but you can only make that choice if you talk about the subject of children beforehand.

The thing is, don't blind side each other with your preferences regarding children. Have this conversation early on. Dating is meant to be trying to find your spouse, so you need to have all of these conversations.

Read Psalm 127: 3-5: "***Lo, children are an heritage of the LORD: and the fruit of the womb is his reward. 4As arrows are in the hand of a mighty man; so are children of the youth. 5Happy is the man that hath his quiver full of them: they shall not be ashamed, but they shall speak with the enemies in the gate.***"

How many children will make your quiver full? That is different for every person, but children are a blessing of God! They are hard work, very hard work! There are ups and downs, but speaking from experience, we are so joyful that we have children. Each of them is so special to us.

However, children are not for everyone. There are many reasons people might have for not wanting children, and it is important to know each other's preferences.

Politics

I covered so many topics without mentioning politics. I thought about not mentioning politics, and I bet you would hope we were not going to mention politics, but here we are: Politics.

This book discusses the Bible and religious topics, so why not include the other "controversial" topic?

Ok. Well, I am not going to say you must affiliate with political party "A" or political party "B." Everyone has their own choice with that, and there are not just two choices; you do not even have to label yourself.

When I was growing up, there were subtle differences with each major political party. Today, it seems like the two main parties are polar opposites. This is unfortunate. It should never get to a place where we belittle a person based on their political (or religious) identity. I know there is an Amendment that covers each of us having freedom related to these topics.

The fact is, you and your spouse may or may not be running for political office, but as you grow up, you will realize that politics impose a large influence on your lives.

Politics affect taxes. Politics influence laws. Politics affect our lives.

It is important to at least talk about issues that are important to you. Talk about what side of the aisle you live on. Are there topics that are not that big a deal to you, or are there topics that you would not change your mind on no matter what?

I have seen political viewpoints affect marriages, but before you say, "Oh, I don't want to deal with politics, I can just follow the Bible and not worry about politics," you should know that the entire Bible revolves around politics too.

Just look at some of the names of the books of the Bible: Judges, I Kings, and II Kings. Now look at some of the people in the Bible: Pharaoh (many different Pharaohs), King Saul, King David, King Herod, all the other Kings, Caesar, and Jesus is the King of Kings. There are honestly so many other examples of politics throughout the Bible. Politics are an important part of the Bible. Politics need to be addressed in your lives.

Are all politicians corrupt? Is everything rigged? Who knows? Maybe. I do not know. What I do know is that we have a voice and need to choose to stand on the right side of politics.

Take a look at 1 Peter 2: 13-14: "**Submit yourselves to every ordinance of man for the Lord's sake: whether it be to the king, as supreme; ¹⁴Or unto governors, as unto them that are sent by him for the punishment of evildoers, and for the praise of them that do well.**"

We are supposed to follow the leaders of our land, and we are supposed to pray for them as well.

Paul writes in 1 Timothy 2: 1-4: "**I exhort therefore, that, first of all, supplications, prayers, intercessions, and giving of thanks, be made for all men; ²For kings, and for all that are in authority; that we may lead a quiet and peaceable life in all godliness and honesty. ³For this is good and acceptable in the sight of God our**

Saviour; ⁴Who will have all men to be saved, and to come unto the knowledge of the truth."

Here it is. It seems pretty spelled out for us. We need to pray for those who lead our nation so we can have a peaceful life. And did you catch that last part: *God would want all people to be saved!* This includes politicians. We need to be praying for their guidance and their salvation.

And just as a side note, God wants you to be saved too! We are praying for everyone who reads this book to come to know Jesus Christ as their own personal Lord and Savior. If you want to know how to get saved, put a bookmark here, and go to the last chapter where we show the way to be saved.

What about politicians that want nothing to do with God? It says in Acts 5:29b: "**We ought to obey God rather than men.**"

Yes, we should obey the government unless it goes against what God teaches us. We have an obligation to obey God instead of man. Do you remember the story of Shadrach, Meshach, and Abednego from Daniel 3? Go back and read this. This story shows how God truly does bless those who decide to obey God rather than man.

Maybe you do not think we are at the point where politics are making you go against God (we believe there are many examples of this already). There will be a day when the government will be in total control, and we will not be able to buy or sell unless we follow them completely.

If you do not know about this time, go ahead and read Revelation Chapter 13.

So I think that I established the idea that politics are important in our lives. But you do not need to make this topic your first conversation with each other. The topic of politics is not exactly the most romantic topic when getting to know each other, but it is important to discuss those political issues that are very important to you, so you do not waste anyone's time and so each of you can know where the other stands.

3   Looking for What You Want

Ok. So now you know what you want in your marriage. Well, that was the easy part. They say that knowing is half the battle, but I think that knowing is even less than half the battle. Now, you must go and look for what (and whom) you know you want; that is not always very easy. Finding "The One" is not so simple to do.

Of course, we all know of those people who were their first crush, fell in love in high school, and have been married for at least 50 years. I love hearing about and talking to these couples. I think that these stories are very special.

But this is definitely not the case for everyone. The 2021 marriage rate is 33.2 per 1000; the Coronavirus divorce rate is 44.8%, up from 44.6% pre-Covid. The average marriage in the US is 8 years, which reflects 7 years of cohabitation and the usual or average one year for a divorce.

My wife and I went to the same high school, but I never said that we were high school sweethearts. We both dated other people before we found each other.

Either scenario is fine. Some people get lucky with the first person; others have to look around for a while before finding someone. And to be honest, sometimes that search helps you find comfort in the person you find.

For my wife and me, we have always said that if one of us never dated anyone else, and the other dated like we did; we probably would not have stayed with each other. For us, it was the similar stories and experiences that we had that made each other appreciate where we came from. Without having that experience, it would have been difficult to understand the other person's past.

This is how it was for my wife and me. This is not how it is for everyone. Some people are more understanding; for some people, it does not matter at all.

The search is what makes the find so much more rewarding for me.

Because of this, you need to know where to look to find what you want.

Shop where they would be

Ok, so this sounds very obvious, but it is important. Oftentimes, this is something that is ignored by many people.

I guess by now you've realized that I like to use examples, so here's another one: If you are looking to buy some strawberries, you should not be going to a big box remodeling store to find those strawberries.

Similarly, if you want a spouse who loves serving the Lord, you probably should not try to find them at a bar. Has there ever been a reported sign of a Christian going to a bar? Yes. No one is perfect, but it would be even harder to find that Christian in a bar.

So where does that leave us? Does that mean you can only find your spouse at church? No, but church is a very good option for finding someone. There are many Christians who go there, your chances would be higher at finding someone there, but it is not a foolproof option. You still have to search.

If your biggest passion in life is books, then perhaps you should try to find your future spouse in a library or a popular bookstore, if those exist anymore.

You need to be looking for the person you want in places where that person can be found. You know what you want, so you will know where to look. You are also going to know where not to look. For example, don't waste your time looking for someone at a ball game if you hate sports.

Now, let's go back to the fresh produce example. I would probably never eat fruit from a gas station (unless I'm on a very long road trip); I would eat produce from a big box grocery store, but I would most prefer to eat produce from a nice farmers' market.

I am not the perfect example for this area either though; both my wife and I have previously looked for people in places where we really would not want to meet someone. Fortunately, we both realized those places were not for us, and we finally started looking in the places where we would want to find someone.

My biggest concern was to find a Christian girl, so I made that my first question, my first requirement when looking for a girl. Instead of looking for someone, getting to know them, and then later asking how they felt about Jesus, I decided to make that my first question.

But it is not just enough to randomly look in the places where you would want to find someone, you need to be in those places so that person can find you.

If you are trying to find someone at church, you need to be going to church regularly. This will allow you to really get to know some people. If you do not go regularly, you might be viewed just like that gas station produce, someone who just cares a little bit about Jesus. You need to be like the farmer's market produce that shows you really love Jesus.

Oh, and that brings me to another point. It must be genuine! I will get back to that.

Please do not think I am saying you can only find someone at church; I am not saying that. You can meet someone at college, at work, at a store, at a park, or so many other places. In fact, please do not feel pressured -- and don't give pressure to other people -- to find someone at church or at Christian college. We know people who went to Christian college to major in finding a spouse.

Sometimes that worked. Sometimes it did not work. Sometimes that farmers' market is all sold out of a certain produce. (Sorry, but sometimes I just keep running with the analogy and strawberries are in season). But honestly, do not set yourself up for failure by resolving that you "must" find someone at a specific place.

Now, let's go back to the idea of being genuine. It will not help anyone if you fake being a certain way, or if you find out someone else was faking being a certain way.

Jesus says in Matthew 7:16: "**Ye shall know them by their fruits. Do men gather grapes of thorns, or figs or thistles?**"

(Ha. See! There was a reason why I kept using the fresh fruit analogy!) Make sure you give it enough time to see the other person's fruits, don't just give a quick glance at the outward appearance.

There are those examples in which people went to church with each other throughout the time they were dating, but once they got married, one person stopped going to church because that's not who they honestly were.

Tricking someone like this will not result in the couple being truly happy. This brings us to the next topic of not wasting each other's time.

Don't waste time with others

If you waste time with others, you are also wasting your own time.

This topic can be taken two ways: Do not waste time with people by misleading them, and also, do not waste time by not going after what you know you want.

First, let's talk about not misleading people.

God said in Leviticus 19:11: "***Ye shall not steal, neither deal falsely, neither lie one to another.***"

This verse is from the part of the Bible known as The Ten Commandments. The Bible also mentions how deceiving people is an abomination to the Lord. (An abomination is an outrage, disgrace, scandal, revulsion).

Would you want someone to mislead you into thinking they were someone they were not? The truth will come out, and feelings will get hurt.

In those exchanges, you are investing time that eventually gets wasted. More important, you are also investing your heart, and that ends up getting broken as soon as the rug gets pulled out from under you. It's not good for either person when someone misleads the other person into thinking they are someone else.

Now let's talk about not going after what you know you want.

Let's say that you found someone genuine that you like, and they like you. It is good to keep getting to know that person and find out more about them, but eventually you need to make the choice whether you want to marry that person or not.

Have you ever known someone who has been dating for 10 or more years? We know people like this. Honestly, I do not even know how the relationship lasts that long. At some point, people usually say to the other person that they need to do something or get off the pot, either propose to get married, or break up and move on.

Staying with someone that long without the intention of ever getting married is also another way of wasting people's time.

Look at Ephesians 5:15-17: "**See then that ye walk circumspectly, not as fools, but as wise, 16Redeeming the time, because the days are evil. 17Wherefore be ye not unwise, but understanding what the will of the Lord is.**"

The Bible tells us not to be foolish about wasting time. You need to look for what you want and understand what the will of the Lord is for you.

Once you find it, do not waste each other's time by not getting married. If you waste time and ignore that aspect, the other person might start thinking they are not what you are looking for, and they will want to start looking other places for someone else.

Be honest

Be honest! I touched on this already when mentioning not to waste each other's time but being honest goes much further than merely that. What I mean here is being honest about everything.

If there is something that deeply bothers you, be honest. Tell the other person. Either it will become a deal breaker, or it can be something that a simple change can fix.

Maybe chewing with your mouth open, or not putting the toothpaste cap back on drives you absolutely mad. If so, work that into a conversation. To me, these would not be a deal breaker, but if something bothers you, it should be addressed. At the very least, you will avoid building up so much resentment and anger from years of "tolerating" that one bad habit your spouse has.

Recall Jesus saying in Matthew 18:15: "***Moreover if thy brother shall trespass against thee, go and tell him his fault between thee and him alone: if he shall hear thee, thou hast gained thy brother.***"

The Bible tells us to talk to someone if they offend us, and we are told that this will help us build a stronger and healthier relationship with each other.

Refer to Matthew 7:3-5: "***And why beholdest thou the mote that is in thy brother's eye, but considerest not the beam that is in thine own eye? ⁴Or how wilt thou say to thy brother, Let me pull out the mote out of thine eye; and, behold, a beam is in thine own eye? ⁵Thou hypocrite, first cast out the beam out of thine own eye; and then shalt thou see clearly to cast out the mote out of thy brother's eye.***"

Even though we are instructed to talk about faults and issues that bother us, we need to remember to check ourselves for any faults or issues that we might have. We ought to understand that we might be doing some things that also drive our spouse equally crazy. So when they approach you about something, try to understand where they are coming from and try to grow from there.

Being honest, though, does not just mean telling each other what bothers you; it means you remember to say those things delicately so you are not mean and hurt each other's feelings.

Being honest also means to not hide things from each other.

First, we know that we are not able to hide ours sins forever. Our sins will catch up to ourselves, and God will always know all our sins. It is better to just be open and honest at first with your spouse before they find things out down the road.

Some of the consequences are in Numbers 32:23: "***But if ye will not do so, behold, ye have sinned against the LORD: and be sure your sin will find you out.***"

You might try to hide things from your spouse, but you will never be able to hide things from God. On a side note though, remember that if we confess our sins, God will forgive all of our sins. This is found in I John 1:9, and we need to repent of our sins if we want to be saved:

I John 1:9: "*If we confess our sins, he is faithful and just to forgive us our sins, and to cleanse us from all unrighteousness.*"

If you hide things from your spouse, it will set up your marriage to have holes in it that will lead to an unstable foundation in your marriage.

See Proverbs 28:13: "*He that covereth his sins shall not prosper: but whoso confesseth and forsaketh them shall have mercy.*"

Sure, some things from your past might not be your most prideful memories, but it is better to be honest right away with that information, before your spouse finds out about it on their own.

You might think you are trying to protect each other from that information, but really what you are doing is creating the premise that you hide other information from your spouse. And then what? What else are you hiding? How can you be trusted now? Once trust is broken, it is very difficult to rebuild.

Being honest, though, does not mean you should not try to go outside your comfort level to impress each other.

For me, this is a simple example. When my wife and I were dating, she loved drinking coffee and I never liked it. I never went out of my way to say, "Hey, let's go get coffee."

But there were a few times my wife asked if I wanted to get coffee with her, and I replied with "I guess I will have some."

Looking back at it, I might not have conveyed my absolute dislike for coffee adequately. Since we were dating, I haven't had a sip of coffee at all, and I definitely do not miss it at all.

We are not perfect, that is for sure. I could have done a much better job at letting my wife know how much I did not like coffee. Fortunately for us, this was not a huge deal that affected our marriage at all, although I still sometimes forget about the "need" to stop and get coffee on the way to church on Sunday mornings when we are rushing to not be late.

In any case though, be honest with each other. You will want your spouse to have the ability to be their complete comfortable self without having to worry about hiding something from you, so return the favor by being your complete comfortable self without hiding anything from your spouse.

Be open and vulnerable

Being open and vulnerable goes that step further than being honest.

When you are honest with each other, you do become vulnerable. Maybe you are vulnerable for the other person to reject you for what you just shared. But you are also vulnerable for the other person to increase the amount of trust they have in you and between you.

Being open can include a lot of different topics. One example is whether you want to move out of the state in which you live, and you want to share that information with your spouse. Before you share that information, you might not know if they would share your interests.

On the other side of the example, you should try to be open and vulnerable to try new things, maybe like move out of state with your spouse. For this example, your job might be a reason you would not want to move, but maybe you can travel with your job. Even if you can't work remotely, maybe you can find a similar job in a new state.

Remember, you are in this relationship forever, but you will retire one day from your job. You shouldn't have to bend over backwards to make your employer happy with you. You should look out for you and your spouse first to make sure you are supporting the best life you can have.

You don't have to try everything that is new but maybe a few things. You will never know what you do and don't like until you try it. Try to be open and vulnerable with each other throughout your marriage.

Being open and vulnerable also means that you are not perfect. You will make mistakes. Even if you are saved, you will continue to fall.

Paul wrote in Romans 6:23: "***For all have sinned, and come short of the glory of God;***"

We are all sinners and need forgiveness from God.

Take a look at I John 1:9: "***If we confess our sins, he is faithful and just to forgive us our sins, and to cleanse us from all unrighteousness.***"

Confessing our sins or faults and asking God for forgiveness is the only way to gain forgiveness of our sins.

Just as God already knows each and every sin that we commit, but He wants us to confess our sins and ask for forgiveness before He forgives us, your spouse already knows you are not perfect and wants to hear you admit not just the good but the bad, too, so they can forgive and accept you.

In today's age of technology, tracking, and tracing capabilities, there is no hiding anything from anyone. Big government, Big Tech, and all of the other "Bigs" can find out every detail of your life; there probably is a camera always recording us (especially if we have "smart" devices).

I know this is not at the same level of what God knows about us, but we should always be ready to be held accountable for our actions. Whether we are accountable to our spouse, or accountable to God, we need to know that we should not try to hide anything from our spouse or God.

When you become married, you become one flesh with that person, just as it states in Mark 10:7-8: "***For this cause shall a man leave his father and mother, and cleave to his wife; ⁸And the twain shall be one flesh: so then they are no more twain, but one flesh.***"

Since you are one flesh, why would you even try to hide anything from your spouse.

4   Finding What You Want

Now that you know what you want, and you know what to look for in a spouse, now you need to find what you want. Finding what you want, except that is not as easy as choosing what kind of ice cream you want to have.

Ice cream is certainly not the best comparison here; ice cream is something that will not last that long, especially depending on how much you enjoy ice cream.

One example that comes to mind is when you need to find a car. I think it is safe to generalize here, but I will speak only for myself. When I shop for a car, I will not simply pick the first car I see. I will look for the types of cars I want before I even go look at the car I pick out.

I won't jump the gun.

I will take my time making sure that the car measures up to what was advertised. If it is as good as I think it is, I will not wait too long before going through the process to make that car belong to me.

Once I choose the perfect car for me, I will make sure I actually like it and what it has to offer. I will enjoy my time driving around with my new car.

Finally, I will have to figure out the car. It is not a perfect car. There is necessary upkeep, maintenance, and care to keep the car in good condition.

Before you read any further, you know your spouse is not a car. Do not get a new one every year or so, and do not have multiple ones at a time!

Look at Matthew 19:4-5: "***And he answered and said unto them, Have ye not read, that he which made them at the beginning made them male and female, 5And said, For this cause shall a man leave father and mother, and shall cleave to his wife: and they twain shall be one flesh?***"

And once you become the one flesh, you should love one another as your own self.

Paul wrote in Ephesians 5:29-31: "***For no man ever yet hated his own flesh; but nourisheth and cherisheth it, even as the Lord the church: 30For we are members of his body, of his flesh, and of his bones. 31For this cause shall a man leave his father and mother, and shall be joined unto his wife, and they two shall be one flesh.***"

We are supposed to love our own body and treat it with the most respect and care.

Take a look at I Corinthians 6:19-20: "***What? know ye not that your body is the temple of the Holy Ghost which is in you, which ye have of God, and ye are not your own? 20For ye are bought with a price: therefore glorify God in your body, and in your spirit, which are God's.***"

Your body is not your body. Your body is a vessel that is to be used for God's glory. When you are saved, Christ lives in you, He lives in your heart. Therefore, your body is a temple in which God lives, and we need to honor and treat our bodies with complete reverence.

What exactly does that mean? How do you do that?

I can go into the controversial topic of tattoos and piercings, which are addressed in the Bible. (Leviticus 19:28 and Ezekiel 16:12 just to name two verses), but what I really want to say on this point is that you should treat your body as you would treat something you hold with the highest amount of respect.

For me, this is why I TRY to eat healthy but I am not perfect on this point, either. I do know that I do not feel healthy or good after eating junk food. The fake ingredients and chemicals that make our "food" today leave me wondering what we are even eating. So often I see advertisements describing how certain foods or ingredients are linked to causing cancer, Parkinson's disease, or other illnesses.

Besides not feeling good when I eat that fake food, I do not want to end up with some health condition because of the food I ate. So we make an effort to eat healthy, natural food. We try our best to grow some of our food in our little garden at home and try to get the rest of our food at the local farmers' market.

Again, I am nowhere close to perfect or at a level where I can brag about how healthy I eat, but I do know that I need to treat my body with respect and not be a glutton either.

Paul made this clear in I Corinthians 10:31: "***Whether therefore ye eat, or drink, or whatsoever ye do, do all to the glory of God.***"

Since we are to treat our own bodies with respect and care, we need to also treat our spouse's body with respect and care, because those who are married are one flesh.

Not only should we treat each other with respect for this reason, but there's more: Men, you need to love your wife just as Christ loves the church.

See Ephesians 5:25: "***Husbands, love your wives, even as Christ also loved the church, and gave himself for it***,"

Each man is charged with loving his wife in this way because they are the ordained leader of their marriage, as it states:

Ephesians 5:23-24: "***For the husband is the head of the wife, even as Christ is the head of the church: and he is the saviour of the body. 24 Therefore, as the church is subject unto Christ, so let the wives be to their own husbands in everything.***"

And since Christ is the head of the church, we need to submit unto Christ. For this reason, the wife should also submit unto her husband and his leadership.

Some people get thrown off by the phrases about love and submission, but you cannot truly love unless you respect, and you cannot truly respect unless you submit. We will get into this in more detail later in this book.

So back to the idea of finding what you want. You have to make sure not to jump the gun, but don't wait too long; have fun, and figure each other out.

Don't jump the gun

Everyone has heard the old expression that only fools rush in, correct? Well, it is actually a good idea not to rush into marriage. Remember, marriage is something that is supposed to last a lifetime.

It is great that you know what you want to look for, and you even know where to look, but do not stress out about the great desire to find your spouse right this second. Just as the other steps were a process that needed to be addressed with care, finding what you want must also be approached with care.

Just because you know what you want and know where to look, that does not mean that your future spouse is ready. They might not know what they want yet, and they might not be ready for a big commitment.

This just means that maybe you shouldn't immediately ask them if they are ready to marry you five seconds after meeting each other for the first time.

I do know of couples who discussed marriage very early on in their relationships and got married very quickly. Some couples get married within a few months of when they started to date each other.

This is great when it works out. It just means that both people were exactly on the same page and ready for the next step with each other. Yet during the overwhelming majority of the time, each person needs some time to realize whether they are what each other is looking for.

This is a feeling and an experience that happens, and there is no exact script you need to follow for how long you get to know each other. But to be safe, give each other time to figure each other out, and find out if the other person is truly the one for which you were looking.

When I talk to young couples or individuals who are in search of their spouses, I tell them that it is a good idea to date for a while until they get married. I don't mean years and years of dating, even though that is necessary for some people.

I think it is important to find out who it is you are truly dating before getting married. Most of the time, people put on their best show and appearance when they go on dates. This is great and expected; you should put in effort to impress each other.

It states in I Samuel 16:7: "***But the LORD said unto Samuel, Look not on his countenance, or on the height of his stature; because I have refused him: for the LORD seeth not as man seeth; for man looketh on the outward appearance, but the LORD looketh on the heart.***"

Ok. If you know your Bible, you know that this verse is not talking about dating or anything like that. It does show, however, the point of how we tend to only focus on the outward appearances. We need to be like Christ and look at the inward person to find out who the real person is.

Impressing each other is a great thing for relationships because it admittedly feels really good. It is a great feeling when you are on an extravagant date with every circumstance planned to perfection, but this is not how life is every day.

Marriage deals with the good and the bad times. When you get married, you are going to see each other in less than perfect situations. You will see each other sick, sad, or mad. There are endless situations that you can encounter in your life, and it is impossible to experience all of those situations before getting married.

So when I give advice to people, I say that they should try to date and wait for marriage until they experience some big events together. For some people, that might be going through the Christmas season with each other. Unfortunately, a lot of people have some family drama that shows itself around Thanksgiving or Christmas. This time of the year is also a popular time for people to meet each other's extended families.

And oftentimes when a lot of family members get together, you might witness some drama. This is a great time to see how each other handles family stress. This is an indicator of how each of you will deal with stress in the family you create together.

Maybe you find that person is a true champ and handles themselves quite honorably and with compassion. Other times, you might witness an anger-filled explosion when the other person reacts to the drama. Or maybe you find out something that you never knew before that is just a deal-breaker. Whatever the circumstances, you will find out more about each other during these situations. Other times that are good to witness are any times that bring out the real person who is behind those perfect dates.

I am not saying that you need to date through at least one Christmas to ensure a successful marriage. You can have good discussions and witness telling signs at any point during the dating phase.

See Psalm 27:14: "***Wait on the LORD: be of good courage, and he shall strengthen thine heart: wait, I say, on the LORD.***"

Marriage is a vow made before the Lord Jesus Christ, so He will let you know His will. Be patient. Keep praying for the Lord to show you His path for you. If you do this, God will give you the courage and strength to continue your path. Do not rush things, and God will take care of your heart.

Don't wait too long

Now that I went into detail explaining how you need to make sure that you don't rush into a marriage, I will also say that you need to make sure that you do not wait too long before you get married.

You should not wait forever to find out if that person is the person you are meant to marry. If you keep waiting to make your decision, the other person might end up feeling that you do not think they are valuable or worth marrying. They might decide to just break it off with you and find someone else if you never get to that point where you say you want to spend your life together.

Everyone knows at least one couple that has been dating for over a decade or engaged for over a decade, but never actually got married. Maybe these people have discussed this issue, and they are both okay with that situation, but oftentimes I have seen where one of them ends up questioning why the other never wanted to marry them.

Some of these people will list their reasons why they will not marry yet. They are waiting for some elusive scenario for them to get married. Yet if you plan to stay together and never break up, why would you not want to honor your relationship and make a promise before each other and God that you will always love each other?

There will always be events in your life that will be less than perfect; but when you are married, at least you have each other to help you through everything.

Another reason for not waiting so long to get married can be your age, especially if the plan is to have children. This can be a big influential factor. Raising children is hard work, and it is even harder when you start raising a child at an older age. Children are very active, and it is very natural to want to participate and be active with your children. Also, it becomes physically more difficult to have a baby as you get older.

This topic of having children will not apply to everyone; not everyone will want to have children. Maybe you just do not want children, are too nervous about raising a child in this world, or you are too old to have one. In any case, this might not be a deciding factor for you.

My wife and I always wanted to have a big family. We did not get married when we were young or old, but we did want to start growing our family soon after we got married, and that is what we did. We had four children in the first four years of our marriage, because we wanted to still be relatively young as our children grew up. And having our children has been a real blessing to our lives, as well.

Another reason to not wait too long to get married is the fact that life is short and we never know how long we have.

It says in Proverbs 27:1: "***Boast not thyself of tomorrow; for thou knowest not what a day may bring forth.***"

See Luke 12:20: "***But God said unto him, Thou fool, this night thy soul shall be required of thee: then whose shall those things be, which thou hast provided?***"

We might have all these great plans and desires, but the reality is, we will never know just how long we have to live. Anything can happen at any time. Either your life can be suddenly ended, or your life can be tragically altered forever in a moment. We cannot guarantee anything about our future.

See James 4:14: "***Whereas ye know not what shall be on the morrow. For what is your life? It is even a vapour, that appeareth for a little time, and then vanisheth away.***"

Since our lives are so short and precious, we need to make every moment count. First, we need to live our lives serving the Lord Jesus Christ.

Jesus stated in John 12:26: "***If any man serve me, let him follow me; and where I am, there shall also my servant be: if any man serve me, him will my Father honour.***"

We need to honor God; and then in return, He will honor us.

Second, we need to make good and wise decisions in our lives, and for many people, one of those decisions will be getting married, but marriage is also not for everyone.

See I Corinthians 7:2: "***Nevertheless, to avoid fornication, let every man have his own wife, and let every woman have her own husband.***"

If at very least, one reason to get married is to avoid the sin of fornication.

Paul further wrote in I Corinthians 7:8-9: "***I say therefore to the unmarried and widows, It is good for them if they abide even as I. ⁹But if they cannot contain, let them marry: for it is better to marry than to burn.***"

Here, the Bible talks about how being unmarried can lead to potential sin in your life. In Matthew Chapter 19, the Bible gives us a story in which it can be better to not marry if it would just lead to other sins like adultery.

Jesus Christ himself did not get married, but He had a greater purpose in His life than to be married. Marriage is supposed to be a picture of the relationship we have with Jesus, and there are so many benefits to being married. Just one benefit is that you would have someone to share every good and bad thing with for your entire life, and that can help tremendously.

It is written in Proverbs 18:22: "***Whoso findeth a wife findeth a good thing, and obtaineth favour of the LORD.***"

For me, I wanted to experience some of these benefits and blessings of being married; and it truly has been a blessing throughout my life.

Have fun

Speaking about blessings, you should also have some fun while you find whom you will marry. Even though you need to sign a marriage certificate and pay money for the marriage certificate, that does not mean that dating or marriage should only be a business transaction. In fact, if you approach it that way, it probably will not end well.

Sure, you need to find out all the important information about the other person, and make sure you do not go too slowly, but you also need to make sure not to rush into it either. Besides, you can do all of that finding out in an enjoyable fashion.

Dating is not a formal interview or interrogation. Find everything you need to find out by going out on dates and having comfortable, organic, and unforced conversations.

As I said before, there are some topics that you should probably not talk about on the first date. It's unlikely these topics will even come up naturally on the first few dates anyway, so do not force those issues.

The most fragile part of your dating phase is during the beginning, so do not make the first part awkward or uncomfortable. Enjoy it. Make each other smile.

Trust me, life will only get busier and there will be more responsibilities. My wife and I still make it a priority to go on dates, but with four young children, it is difficult to find the time or a babysitter so we can make time for each other. Nevertheless, this is a priority, and I will get back to that topic later in this book.

Since life will only get busier, take advantage of that; do all the activities and traveling while you are dating. Of course, not all your dates have to be the most expensive or elaborate dates ever. All that matters is that your date is enjoyable for both of you.

Sharing enjoyable dates does not mean you should not put any effort into dating. You want to be impressed, and that means the person you are dating also wants to be impressed. If you do not try, the other person will not feel the need to try, either.

This honestly leaves the door open to almost anything. When I was dating my wife, some of our best and most memorable dates were when we went for hikes. We just went for a nice relaxing car ride to various trails, and then we would hike. It was a peaceful time when we can still talk and get to know each other. Enjoying hiking was something we always had in common. We love to share our enjoyment of being out in nature, seeing some wildlife at times, and just admiring God's creation all around us. In addition, we should take notice of all of God's beautiful creations around us.

This is revealed in Psalm 19:1: "***The heavens declare the glory of God; and the firmament sheweth his handywork.***"

Everything that God created points back to Him and how wonderful and magnificent He is.

As stated in Romans 1:20: "***For the invisible things of him from the creation of the world are clearly seen, being understood by the things that are made, even his eternal power and Godhead; so that they are without excuse:***"

Just by observing God's handiwork and creations, we can witness His eternal power. From this, we can realize and understand that without God, there would be nothing; we would know that everything is because of God. From that realization, we have no excuse; we should seek more knowledge of who made everything, who God is, what He has done and still does for us, and how we can be with Him for all eternity?

The answer to all those insights and awareness rests in a verse that so many people know already:

John 3:16: "***For God so loved the world, that he gave his only begotten Son, that whosoever believeth in him should not perish, but have everlasting life.***"

This verse is self-explanatory, but just to make sure you know what it means in its fullest sense, Christ died for everyone's sins, and if we believe in Him, we can be with Him forever. I will explain this more at the end of this book.

Back to dating. My wife and I also went out to eat a lot for some dates. You can play games or share any enjoyable, activity. The basic rule for dating is to have fun. Hopefully, you will spend your entire life with each other, so you should learn how to have fun with each other.

Let me just touch on one other topic here. Try to limit yourself to having clean and pure fun.

I know. This might be more of an awkward reference, so I have tried to make this quick. Regardless, you need to address this topic.

Some people out there have extremely strict guidelines to follow when dating, like no holding hands, they must have a chaperone, or other safety precautions. I am not saying you should or should not do any of these things. I am saying that you should try to hold each other accountable for what God tells us to do and how to conduct ourselves.

The rules are clear even just in the Ten Commandments (Exodus 20:1-17).

Paul wrote in Hebrews 13:4: "***Marriage is honourable in all, and the bed undefiled: but whoremongers and adulterers God will judge.***"

Try to stay pure before getting married. This is what God tells us to do, but in abiding by this, you also will see real world benefits. If you rush into the sexual side of a relationship before getting married, it can indicate that the other person is not worth the wait. It can also be interpreted to mean the other person and their personality are not good enough for you so you need to have more to even want to stay with that person.

Other things can happen, too, like getting pregnant long before either of you is ready to have any children.

I do know that not everyone follows this, and I also know that God can forgive anything. Still, remember that there is a price and consequence for everything.

Look at Numbers 32:23: "***But if ye will not do so, behold, ye have sinned against the LORD: and be sure your sin will find you out.***"

Also, let me be honest; all of us will get old and less attractive in life. There will come a time when your relationship will revolve around the physical. You need to have a solid relational foundation to know that the two of you can stand the test of time.

So make sure to have fun while you date, but make sure that the fun you have is good, clean fun. Make sure you do all of this so that you can better figure each other out, and that brings up the next topic.

Figure each other out

At this point, you could think that you already might have completely figured out one another. However, figuring each other out is an ongoing process that takes time and effort.

Remember, you are doing this not just for yourself, but because the other person will be in your life for the rest of their life too. So you need to try to figure out one another so both of you will be completely happy.

You spent all this time to find out what you want and what will make you happy, but you also must make sure you find out what the other person's interests, fears, and desires are. A marriage is not a one way street where whatever you want will happen. If this were the case, you would end up in a head-on collision, since you are both going your own way on that street.

Life and marriage are about compromise, but I am not saying that you should compromise your own integrity or standards just to end up with that person. I am saying that you do not always have to have your own way.

I absolutely hate seafood. In fact, I am actually allergic to seafood, but I know that my wife loves seafood. If I had it my way, I would never step foot in a seafood restaurant, but doing that would deprive my wife of something she really enjoys. If my wife had it her way, she would eat seafood maybe five days out of the week, and this would make me very sick. So we both try to care for each other and do what the other one wants. My wife tries not to eat that much seafood, but I also do not try to stop her from ordering it whenever we are at a restaurant.

Now, if I just focused on my needs and desires, I would only know that I can't eat seafood. If I never figured out my wife, I never would have found out she loves it.

Take a look at I Corinthians 8:13: "***Wherefore, if meat make my brother to offend, I will eat no flesh while the world standeth, lest I make my brother to offend.***"

In this passage, we see a similar example. This passage can be talking about someone with a very bad allergy. I know of some married couples who never eat or have any nut products in their house because their spouse is deathly allergic to nuts. Or this passage can also refer to anything that can offend or bother someone; it is not just limited to eating or not eating something. This passage refers to anything that can offend someone, especially if it would hurt their Christian walk.

But figuring each other out does not limit you only to finding out what not to do; figuring each other out should also mean finding out what each of you like.

Jesus said in Matthew 7:12: "***Therefore all things whatsoever ye would that men should do to you, do ye even so to them: for this is the law and the prophets.***"

Here, the Bible tells us that we need to treat each other the way that we want to be treated.

You want to be treated specially, so naturally, your spouse will want to be treated specially as well. Pay attention to their desires and needs. Don't always do just the things that you like, but keep dating each other and making each other feel special.

See Acts 20:35: "***I have shewed you all things, how that so labouring ye ought to support the weak, and to remember the words of the Lord Jesus, how he said, It is more blessed to give than to receive.***"

The Bible tells us that it is better to give and do special things for other people than it is for us to be on the receiving end all the time.

I do admit that it feels great when my wife does something nice for me, but it is such a better feeling to see how good it makes my wife feel when I do something nice for her.

The only way you can keep the spice alive is to constantly find out more about each other and actively try to do nice things for each other.

Obviously, this does not only mean you have to spend money on each other; this mostly means the ways that you care for each other and the gestures and attention you give each other every day… and this is an everyday thing. Don't stop trying. You are each other's most prized possession. Take care of each other and value each other's desires.

And if you realize that you value each other so much, then the next step will be the next topic, which is getting married.

5   Tying the Knot

Getting married, or "tying the knot," is the next step in your relationship. It is the event that symbolizes that you are making the lifelong commitment and covenant with each other.

This event is different in so many cultures, and how you get married is up to you. Some people go all out and spend endless amounts of money on the wedding. Hey, if you can afford it and want this type of wedding, then enjoy it. Other people cannot be that ostentatious with the ceremony, and they will only do a signing of a paper at the courthouse with a witness or two. In some cultures, the wedding takes a couple hours, while in other cultures, the wedding lasts a few days.

Whatever you decide, make sure it is something that the two of you want, like, and can do. The wedding day is only about the two of you (Really it's her day!) Do not let other people dictate what you should do or how you should celebrate your special time.

This is your special time

This is your special time, not your great aunt's or your best friend's from work. Let's face it, you worked hard to get here. You both did. Countless hours and dedication went into trying to find the perfect spouse. Your wedding is your special time that will stand out in your memory; your wedding is the time your two lives merged into one life.

I know that in my relationship, I was working my clinical rotation at the hospital for at least 12 hour days, every day of the week. At the end of each day, I drove another hour (if there was no traffic) to hang out and maybe get some food with my now wife. I ended up getting very few hours of sleep every day, but this was my investment to make sure I found the perfect girl, and I did! So when it was time for our wedding, we went "all out."

Well, to be honest, we went as "all out" as we were reasonably able to do. And that is what is important. There is no guidebook that says what you "need" to do when planning a wedding. Really all you need is that little piece of paper filled out and signed by the town hall in which you are getting married.

This is a special day, so many people try to have some type of celebration for it. I agree that it is a great thing to do, and I understand there might be certain other situations, or finances, that make it difficult, but having some kind of ceremony is very special.

The ceremony does not have to include thousands of people or people that you barely know. A good idea is to make it only for those who are most important to you. This could be your close family and friends.

Throughout the Bible there are passages about doing things as a memorial to certain events:

Exodus 12:14: "***And this day shall be unto you for a memorial; and ye shall keep it a feast to the LORD throughout your generations; ye shall keep it a feast by an ordinance forever.***"

This passage references the children of Israel and one of the many times they were told to mark a day and remember it throughout their lives.

It states in Genesis 29:21-22: "***And Jacob said unto Laban, Give me my wife, for my days are fulfilled, that I may go in unto her. ²²And Laban gathered together all the men of the place, and made a feast.***"

In this passage, Jacob worked seven years at this time before being able to marry Rachel. At the end of the seven years, Rachel's father gathered many people and put together a large feast to celebrate their marriage.

Unfortunately, in this story Rachel's father tricked Jacob and gave him his other daughter to marry, so Jacob had to wait another seven years before he could finally marry Rachel.

What I am saying is that you are working hard to get to the point of marriage, so you earned a little special celebration with each other.

Celebrate your wedding in a way that is special to the two of you. Do not worry about someone else saying what would be nice to them. Your wedding day is a day for your guests to celebrate your happiness, not a day to make your guests happy.

Remember that your wedding day is for you and not for them. They probably will not remember what you had for food, the colors of the bridesmaids' dresses, or even your wedding day. All of this is what makes it special for the two of you, and you will be the ones remembering those details. Well, please try to remember at least the date of your wedding.

This brings us to the next point: Make it memorable.

Make it memorable

Your wedding is a special day in your life. There are many special memories that you will make throughout your life with your spouse, and hopefully you will be able to remember most of these precious moments, but chances are, your memory will fade and you will not recall every single memory.

This is the reason you should make an extra effort to make this day special. Even though you might have already promised before each other and God that you will always love each other and be together, your wedding is an outward show to let each other and friends and family know that you are vowing yourselves to each other before God.

Plan and do things that are important to both of you. Whether it is the vows that you say, the decorations, or the people you invite, you need to absorb everything that happens that day.

It might be stressful planning and coordinating, but when the day comes, it will go by quickly.

If you are able, take pictures and videos of your wedding, but don't just stop there. Look through the pictures and watch the video once in a while. Yes, you might already remember it, but there is something special about re-living that day.

My wife and I have wedding pictures displayed in our bedroom, and we try to watch our wedding video about once a year. It always makes us smile.

Let's say you can't afford to take pictures or record video. A good way to remember your wedding it is to tell your story often.

This is something that my wife and I often do too, especially when we meet a new couple and start hanging out with them. We ask them how they met, how the proposal went, and how their wedding was. We always share our stories too. It is a simple and free way to relive your greatest most special memories and hear about other people's experiences.

As we read in Exodus 12:14 before, "it is important to tell and remind our future generations as an eternal commemoration of the important events in our lives."

Even though you might do a quiet little courthouse signature to get married, it is a good idea to have a special ceremony to remember what took place in your lives.

Just like after you get saved, you would walk forward at church and let people know that you got saved.

See Matthew 28:19: "***Go ye therefore, and teach all nations, baptizing them in the name of the Father, and of the Son, and of the Holy Ghost:***"

We are also told to get baptized after we get saved as a way to showcase and memorialize the event of salvation. Baptism is a way to celebrate your salvation.

Celebrate it

When you make your wedding meaningful and memorable, you will naturally want to celebrate it.

As we know, people typically celebrate their wedding on their wedding day, but also people should, at the very least, celebrate their wedding anniversary every year. This is done to remember the day, to show how and why you fell in love, and to help preserve and rekindle the love you have for each other.

Of course, you celebrate your marriage on your wedding day, but your marriage is not over after your wedding day, so the celebration should never end either.

Yes, the annual anniversary of your wedding is a perfect time to celebrate your marriage. This gives you a chance to show each other that you still love each other and how you love each other.

Remembering to celebrate your marriage is a way to let your spouse know that you still cherish them, as they do, too.

Again, it is not about the money and cost to celebrate. Of course, sometimes some anniversary plans can become expensive, and it is a nice gesture to save up money for when the day comes that you can spoil your spouse. Yet it does not always have to be an elaborate celebration. It could be a quiet getaway or just valuable, uninterrupted time together. You can do something that you used to do when you were dating, or you can do something that you always wanted to do.

It does not really matter what you do, but make sure that you are celebrating. Don't forget to make it about the two of you and feel free to talk and reminisce about your wedding or your dating life with each other.

Don't rush through your celebration. Life moves too quickly as it is, and if you have children, try to get someone to watch the kids so you can really make your celebration all about the two of you and you can celebrate your marriage.

My wife and I try to go on a family vacation with the kids every year, but for our anniversary, we always get someone to watch our children as we spend some time to ourselves.

Be creative and meaningful to yourselves in how you celebrate it. You do not have to follow any list that says what to do for each year of marriage, however, it is very fun to make certain years a special celebration. And this can be completely arbitrary, but anniversaries such as the 10-, 20-, 25-, or 50-year anniversary are always fun for you to do something extra special.

But the celebration does not always have to be on the same day either. Being close to the same day is a nice gesture, but sometimes this is not that practical. What matters is that both of you are okay with celebrating your wedding on a different day. My wife and I do this; sometimes we celebrate our anniversary a month or so after our actual anniversary date.

The only reason why I say to try to celebrate your marriage close to your anniversary is because the further away you go from your anniversary, it might feel weird to end up doing nothing on your actual anniversary date.

When my wife and I celebrate our anniversary a month or so after our anniversary, we at least go out to a special dinner on our actual anniversary.

But on another note, you never have to wait for the actual anniversary to celebrate your marriage. Feel free to --

and I encourage you -- to do something special for your spouse randomly throughout the year. This lets them know how much you love them.

Doing something on the actual day is expected, but a random act of kindness is unexpected and very special.

Try just surprising them one day with flowers, card, dinner, a mini vacation, etc. The reaction and reception to this gesture will be incredible.

You should be loving each other your entire lives, so why not show your love to each other at all times too?

This should go without saying, but do not do anything just because you "have to." Do it because you love each other and you want your relationship to blossom. Do it for each other and to keep your relationship healthy and thriving.

Paul wrote in 2 Corinthians 9:7: "***Every man according as he purposeth in his heart, so let him give; not grudgingly, or of necessity: for God loveth a cheerful giver.***"

Yes, this is usually used in reference for giving a tithe to God and the church, but the message still holds true. Celebrate and give gifts out of love, not because you need to do that. God loves a cheerful giver, and God will bless your marriage. Also, your spouse will also love you more if you celebrate your marriage out of love and not out of necessity.

And when we give to God, we are honoring Him; when you give to your spouse, you are honoring them.

Honor it

And honoring your spouse is exactly what we need to be doing. This is a deeper intention than just doing something nice for each other.

The way to honor each other can be seen by learning how to really love each other. First, you need to have more than just a strong like or a lustful admiration towards each other. You need to be loving each other with the same love that Christ has for us.

It is written in Ephesians 5:21-25: "***Submitting yourselves one to another in the fear of God. 22Wives, submit yourselves unto your own husbands, as unto the Lord. 23For the husband is the head of the wife, even as Christ is the head of the church: and he is the saviour of the body. 24Therefore, as the church is subject unto Christ, so let the wives be to their own husbands in everything. 25Husbands, love your wives, even as Christ also loved the church, and gave himself for it;***"

Before anyone gets too upset with the very widely known verse 22, look at verse 21. Both husband and wife are told to submit to each other in the fear of God; or in other words, with respect to God and His commandments. You are one flesh now as a married couple; you are an inseparable team, an everlasting partnership. And in reference to these descriptions, respect, consult, negotiate, submit, and work together with every decision you make in your lives.

Yes, then in verse 22 and 23, we see that the wives should submit themselves to their husbands, and this is a reference to how the husband is the captain of the team, just like God is the head of the church.

And then in verse 24, God says that a wife should follow the guidance of the husband, just as the church needs to follow the guidance of Christ. I am not trying to upset anyone here, but this is what God tells us to do.

A marriage is not a totalitarian dictatorship by the husband though; this would be against what the Bible teaches. The husband and wife need to work together and discuss matters, then the husband will make the final decisions about how he will lead the family, based upon Godly meditation and advice they sought together.

Do not forget that we are told to work together first, then we are told that the husband makes the final decision. And the husbands are also reminded in verse 25 to love your wife just as Christ loves the church and sacrificed Himself for the church. Husbands are told this to keep us in check and to make sure that we don't slip into a dictatorship, making any selfish decision we want.

And it is this love, respect, submission, and honor that we need to have towards our spouse. This love is so pure and real, but you need to really pray and strive to continue loving in this way for your entire marriage.

But this might not happen overnight. When you say, "I do," you might not instantly be at that stage of love. Of course, you need to try to be there, but your love for each other needs to continue growing as time goes on.

If we are supposed to love as Christ loves us, will His love ever decrease? No, of course not. We need to improve our love and grow our love so that we can love like Christ.

You do not want your spouse's love to fade, so continue finding new things you love about each other; never stop falling in love with each other.

This is why I said to make sure you keep celebrating your marriage, because this will help you remember, honor, and grow your love for each other.

In I Corinthians 11:23-29, we see the Lord's Supper and how we need to examine ourselves. When we take part in the Lord's Supper, we are supposed to reflect on our lives and resolve any issues before we take the Lord's Supper. This is done as a way to honor Jesus and recognize His love for us as often as we can do it. So you need to also take the time, once in a while, to reflect on your marriage and get things resolved so that you can better love and honor your spouse.

And when you honor your marriage, you need to make sure you really honor it. Make sure you keep your marriage pure, your eyes pure, your heart pure, and your thoughts pure.

See Proverbs 23:7: "***For as he thinketh in his heart, so is he: Eat and drink, saith he to thee; but his heart is not with thee.***"

Thoughts can wander very easily, more easily than actions, but thoughts are what influence your actions. Be careful. It is not worth throwing away everything just for one brief moment.

It says in Hebrews 11:25: "***Choosing rather to suffer affliction with the people of God, than to enjoy the pleasures of sin for a season;***"

The pleasure of sin only lasts so long, then there is a punishment coming. And to be honest, there are a lot of things that will happen throughout your marriage that might cause some struggle, so you need to be prepared to have the victory and honor your marriage. In the next chapter, we will look at some of those issues that you might face.

6   Navigating a Lot

Like I said, you will face quite a variety of circumstances throughout your marriage. Let's face it, it's a lifetime, so obviously a lot of things will happen. You can plan for some of the things because you know they will be coming.

When my wife and I got married, I was just finishing my clinical rotation and I was not sure where I would be finding a job. We knew that there was a chance for us to stay in our current state, but there was another chance that we might have to move away from our families and relocate to another state.

Ultimately, it was God's will that we were able to stay in our current state, but we were ready for whatever came about in our lives.

See in Proverbs 27:1: "***Boast not thyself of tomorrow; for thou knowest not what a day may bring forth.***"

We can neither know, nor can we predict, what will happen in our lives. We can try to prepare for what we think might happen, but we need to be ready, able to navigate, and deal with anything in life.

There will be good times and bad times, but you need to always have your spouse's back and always keep the Lord first in your lives.

This is in Philippians 4:8: "***Finally, brethren, whatsoever things are true, whatsoever things are*** *honest, whatsoever things are just, whatsoever things are pure, whatsoever things are lovely, whatsoever things are of good report; if there be any virtue, and if there be any praise, think on these things.*"

No matter what happens in your life, deal with the bad, but do not dwell on it. Move on. Only focus on and think about the good.

This is the rest of your life

Maybe you got married when you were 18 or maybe 88; either way your marriage is for the rest of your life.

And throughout your lives, you will have to deal with many different things, but remember, share it all with your spouse. They are there to help you in every situation.

It says in Genesis 2:18: "***And the LORD God said, It is not good that the man should be alone; I will make him an help meet for him.***"

Don't think you need to shoulder all of the stress or headache. Do not keep all of the good to yourselves. You are supposed to be there for each other in every circumstance.

Lots will happen

Like I said, marriage is for the rest of your lives, and a lot of things will be happening during that time.

Deal with it one by one. Life might throw 100 things at you at one time, but make sure you address and take care of each thing one at a time.

You don't want to rush through anything too quickly. If you rush through the bad, you might miss something, and it might just get worse. If you rush through the good, you might miss out on realizing some of the blessings you just experienced.

I really enjoy the song *Count Your Blessings*©. It is a great practice to take a break and number each blessing one by one. This way you won't miss anything.

One of our friends once said that they wrote down their blessings on paper so they can look back on it and remember just how good God is.

And with this same mindset, it might be a good idea to write down all your prayer requests so that you can see how and when they get answered.

The planned

Like I said, there will be some things that you are able to plan throughout your lives. And you should try to make plans.

Read Proverbs 10:5: "***He that gathereth in summer is a wise son: but he that sleepeth in harvest is a son that causeth shame.***"

We know or should know when to plant certain things and when they are ready for us to harvest and eat. This type of planning is good, and God tells us that we are wise when we properly plan for things throughout our lives.

We cannot just go through life without making any precautions or plans.

In marriage, this could be making sure you have life insurance or a good retirement package.

I know that my wife (and myself) does not want me to work for the rest of my life. We would like to be able to retire, spend time with each other and our children (and hopefully grandchildren), and relax. But the only way for us to do that is by carefully planning for retirement and putting away some money right now.

But when we make our plans, we need to make sure that we consider God's will and not just what we want.

Jesus said in Luke 22:42: "***Saying, Father, if thou be willing, remove this cup from me: nevertheless not my will, but thine, be done.***"

Jesus Christ prayed, showing us that we need to pray, asking for God's will to be done in our lives, instead of our will. Even though we might think we know what is best for us, God has the full, complete picture; God's will is always what is best for us.

See in Proverbs 16:9: "***A man's heart deviseth his way: but the LORD directeth his steps.***"

We need to pray and look for what God's will is for our lives. God will direct us in the paths that we must take.

The unplanned

Even though you make plans and provisions and pray for God's will to be done, there will be many times when the unexpected will take place.

See James 4:13-14: Come now, ye that say, "'***Today or tomorrow we will go into such a city, and continue*** *there a year, and buy and sell, and get gain:' ¹⁴Whereas ye know not what shall be on the morrow. For what is your life? It is even a vapour, that appeareth for a little time, and then vanisheth away.*"

We can never know the exact time that our life will end here on Earth. It can be today or years from now. The fact is, you need to be ready for when that day does come. Within a blink of an eye, your life can end, and you will be standing in front of Jesus.

See Luke 12:18-20: "*And he said, This will I do: I will pull down my barns, and build greater; and there will I bestow all my fruits and my goods. ¹⁹And I will say to my soul, Soul, thou hast much goods laid up for many years; take thine ease, eat, drink, and be merry, ²⁰But God said unto him, Thou fool, this night thy soul shall be required of thee: then whose shall those things be, which thou hast provided?*"

When you are dead and gone, sure you can leave all your belongings to your spouse or family, but you can't take anything with you. And the only life insurance policy that is worth it is your eternal life insurance policy.

Where will you spend eternity when you die?

There is a way to know for sure that you are going to Heaven with Jesus for all of eternity. All you need to do is repent of your sins and ask Jesus into your heart to save you. That's it. That's all you've got to do to accept the greatest gift of all. If you want to know more about this, I will go into this more in the last chapter of this book.

The downs

The downs and bad times are sadly unavoidable. They will happen.

Sometimes bad things will happen as a result of what you did, but sometimes bad things are a result of the devil trying you.

Read in I Peter 5:8: "***Be sober, be vigilant; because your adversary the devil, as a roaring lion, walketh about, seeking whom he may devour.***"

The devil wants you to fail. He is looking for someone he can attack and cause to sin.

To defend ourselves, we need to stay in close relation and communication with God; we need to get closer to God. And the way for you to protect yourself in your marriage is to stay in close relation and communication with your spouse; you need to get closer to your spouse.

Communication is such a powerful way to help you through the bad times. Sometimes a lack of communication is the cause of a bad fight in your relationship.

Talk with each other regularly. Don't hold anything a secret. Once you start keeping secrets, your spouse will be on guard and wonder what else you are keeping from them.

When they are having a difficult time, some people like to have their space; but the situation will not get resolved until the two of you talk and deal with it. It's okay to take a breath or two before talking, but make sure you don't wait too long.

It says in Ephesians 4:26: "***Be ye angry, and sin not: let not the sun go down upon your wrath.***"

It's ok to get upset, and it will happen, but we are told not to sin while we are angry. We are also told not to let the sun go down upon our wrath. Here we are told not to let too much time pass before we resolve the issue. Ignoring things and not dealing with problems soon enough can cause bitterness to enter, and this will only lead to more problems.

You are each other's best friends, so you should always think and ask yourself if the fight is worth fighting. A lot of times, issues arise from miscommunication, and no one actually meant any harm. Other times, when someone has clearly committed a fault, that person needs to swallow their pride and apologize.

And when your spouse apologizes, accept it and forgive them.

See Matthew 18:21-22: "*²¹**Then came Peter to him, and said, Lord, how oft shall my brother sin against me, and I forgive him? till seven times? ²²Jesus saith unto him, I say not unto thee, Until seven times: but, Until seventy times seven.*"

This means that you should keep forgiving. Now, let me be clear since we are talking about marriage. One, if they are truly sorry, they will not do that same thing over again.

Second, I know some people will be asking what about if/when they… (fill in your list here).

You could have listed cheating, abuse, or something else very bad.

Matthew 19 and Mark 10 both talk about putting away your spouse, and that is referring to a divorce. The topic of divorce is a touchy subject for many people; divorce affects many people.

Yet the Bible does not say that you should get a divorce for any reason you want. You should not divorce just because they drink directly out of the milk carton or don't clean up after themselves.

Divorce is something else that lasts forever. Think about your actions before you do anything so you don't have to think about a divorce. And if it does get brought up, think about it very carefully. It will affect you for the rest of your lives, and it will affect the lives of your children for the rest of their lives. It is not a joke. Nothing is worth throwing your entire life away and causing something that will ruin so many lives. So cherish your spouse and try to work out all your problems.

Look at Ephesians 4:31-32: "***Let all bitterness, and wrath, and anger, and clamour, and evil speaking, be put away from you, with all malice: 32And be ye kind one to another, tenderhearted, forgiving one another, even as God for Christ's sake hath forgiven you.***"

We are told to get rid of all those bad things, soften our hearts, and forgive as God forgave us.

This passage refers to how Jesus died on the cross and rose again so that God can forgive us of all our sin. And when God forgives us, He doesn't decide one day that He is mad at us again and un-forgives us. So we are told to forgive as God forgives us.

I know that this is not easy to do, but thankfully there are also some good times in a marriage too.

The ups

Let's end this chapter on a happier topic. Let's talk about all the good times that you will have as a married couple.

Hopefully the good times are what make up most of your marriage.

Sometimes you will have to try and arrange things so that you can have a good time; other times you will just find yourself in the middle of a wonderful memory-making moment with your spouse. Both are so special.

I know I mentioned this before, but go ahead and make time to make some good memories. And like I said, this could be anything you want.

The more good memories and fun you have, the happier you will be throughout your marriage.

And if you have children, they will notice this. Remember, you are their example.

See Proverbs 22:6: "***Train up a child in the way he should go: and when he is old, he will not depart from it.***"

Whether you are a good or a bad example, you are an example for your children, and they will most likely follow in your footsteps.

Share the good with each other and with other people, too. Sometimes other couples need that encouragement for how to be happy again.

I have noticed that the more I spend in God's Word and praying to Jesus, the happier I am. And the happier I am, the more difficult it is for me to get in a bad mood.

And this helps when you read and pray by yourself. So guess what happens when you and your spouse also read the Bible and pray to Jesus together? You will find yourselves in better moods, closer to God, and closer to each other.

And this will promote a continuous loop of improving your relationship with each other, with God, and with His Word. The second you stop doing one of those, that loop will start to spiral out of control.

Simply stated, I Thessalonians 5:16: "***Rejoice evermore.***"

We are told to rejoice, and God wants us to be happy. Remember, don't dwell on the bad, instead, constantly look for ways to be happy and make good memories. This is a recipe for helping you keep what you have in your marriage.

7   Keeping What You Got

Staying happy and making good memories are ways that will help you throughout your marriage to stay together and keep what you worked so hard to get.

I can't express how sad I get when I hear of someone I know, or even don't know, who is getting a divorce after decades of being married. I feel, in my marriage, we have encountered so many milestones, good times, and trying times, but our love keeps growing stronger from each experience. I could never imagine throwing it all away.

Regardless of how my and my wife's feelings would be crushed if we were to end our marriage, the lives of our children would be impacted for generations.

It states in Numbers 14:18: "***The LORD is longsuffering, and of great mercy, forgiving iniquity and transgression, and by no means clearing the guilty, visiting the iniquity of the fathers upon the children unto the third and fourth generation.***"

Jesus is merciful and forgiving to those who seek forgiveness, but we are still told that our sin can have effects on our third or fourth generation from us. This means that you should not be selfish with your actions; your actions can affect many people to come.

And you need to consider what you would do after a divorce. Would you just stay alone or would you marry again? Either choice you take will have a ripple effect for the rest of your life.

It's a promise

I firmly believe that you should do everything in your power to honor your marriage and keep your marriage. Remember that it is a vow or a promise that you made to God.

In Ecclesiastes, we are taught about when to and when not to make vows. This passage mainly refers to vowing to pay something or fulfill an agreement:

Ecclesiastes 5:4-5: "***When thou vowest a vow unto God, defer not to pay it; for he hath no pleasure in fools: pay that which thou hast vowed. ⁵Better is it that thou shouldest not vow, than that thou shouldest vow and not pay.***"

I really believe that this teaching applies to when we make a vow in our marriage. In a wedding, you stand in front of witnesses, each other, and God, and you promise to always love each other in every situation.

This is not a promise that you should break.

Look at Mark 10:9: "***What therefore God hath joined together, let not man put asunder.***"

Earthly marriage is supposed to be a representation of our heavenly marriage.

Read in Hebrews 13:5: "***Let your conversation be without covetousness; and be content with such things as ye have: for he hath said, I will never leave thee, nor forsake thee.***"

But God will never leave us. Once we are saved, He will never turn His back on us.

Look at John 10:28: "***And I give unto them eternal life; and they shall never perish, neither shall any man pluck them out of my hand.***"

It is such a comforting feeling to know that God will never leave us. No matter what happens in life, good or bad, God is always there for us. And once life is over, we will be able to spend eternity with God.

With that in mind, wouldn't you want that same level of comfort from your spouse, knowing that they will always be there for you? And that means that you need to provide that same kind of comfort to your spouse, as well.

Dedication

That type of comfort that both of you are giving each other takes a great deal of dedication.

Think about a plaque or a statue you might have seen in a public area. There is usually something there showing that the item was dedicated by someone and in honor of someone.

In my home church, we just put in a nice lawn bench with a plaque that has a dedication on it. That bench is now a permanent fixture to the church grounds. It is something that will not be removed.

The dedication in marriage also needs to be permanent with a strong foundation so that it cannot be removed either.

Hard work

Marriage is not something that happens accidentally. It is a purposeful effort that requires hard work. and just like work, we might not want to work at it all the time.

Since we are alluding to work, let's keep the analogy going. When you first get a new job, it is very exciting. You are so excited for this job you have been trying to get for so long. You need to learn about the job though and figure out how to accomplish certain tasks.

What would happen if you didn't feel like showing up for work, or you started to become less dedicated to your job?

At first, not much would happen. Soon, people would start noticing and talking about it. You might get called into the office or have a performance review. And if you don't start improving, you could be suspended or even terminated.

So yes, for a marriage it is hard work at times. Don't let that be a secret; be prepared to work throughout your marriage. But everyone has those off days at work, so be understanding if your spouse is having an off day. And if it is you having an off day, make sure you go back to work the next day with your "A" game.

Don't wait and let it get to the point where people are talking about your problems. Try to resolve things before you need counseling and try to fix things so you don't end up in a divorce.

But if you do need help, get help.

Number one, the best way to get help is to pray to Jesus and read the Bible. You need to be doing this by yourself and as a couple, too... And never pray or read the Bible like you are trying to put on an act and be better than your spouse.

God and the Bible will speak to both of you. You are a team, and the team has team practices, not just individual practices. The Bible is our play-book; God is the general manager; your pastor is the coach; and your friends and family are the fans cheering you on. (Yes, you've seen that I just really like to make analogies!)

Another part of hard work is to make sure you always communicate with each other. This can be difficult if you have any grudges against each other.

Forgiving

The only way to prevent grudges is to forgive each other. I talked about this before and how we need to give complete forgiveness, just as Christ has forgiven us.

I say this again because if you do not completely forgive and move on, you will likely hold onto a grudge. If you start forming a grudge towards your spouse, you end up building a wall that closes both of you out of your lives.

You would then stop sharing and communicating as much, and your tolerance towards each other would be less.

Forgiveness is not an easy thing to do, but we are all sinners. No one is perfect.

See in Romans 3:10: "***As it is written, There is none righteous, no, not one:***"

Again, marriage is a picture of Christ's love for us. If Christ can forgive all of our wicked ways, we need to be able to forgive each other, as well.

Apologizing

Before you can be forgiven, make sure that you apologize. You can't really resolve anything if you are never actually sorry for the wrong that you did.

The more you fill yourself with devotions and your walk with God, the better it will be for your relationship with your spouse.

See Mark 10:8: "***And they twain shall be one flesh: so then they are no more twain, but one flesh.***"

You are one flesh now, so you shouldn't try to make yourself better than the other person. If you tear down your spouse, you are really tearing yourself down, too.

Paul stated in I Thessalonians 5:11: "***Wherefore comfort yourselves together, and edify one another, even as also ye do.***"

You need the encouragement, and you need to encourage your spouse also.

Don't put yourself up on a pedestal or try to make yourself better than the other person.

Keep dating

A good way to make sure you don't lift yourself up higher than your spouse is to keep dating. Just because you are married doesn't mean you have to stop dating.

I also talked about this before, but dating is so important. Dating just means doing something special with or for each other so that your spouse knows you really cherish them.

Make this a priority. Add it to your calendar. Leave work early sometimes, if you're able.

One more analogy.

Your marriage is a picture of God's love for you. You want God to keep blessing you, taking care of you, and making you feel special throughout your life. So make sure you do all of that for your spouse.

Never let go of that "I can't go another second without seeing you" love. Make sure you also grow your love into "Christ loving the church" love.

See John 3:16: "***For God so loved the world, that he gave his only begotten Son, that whosoever believeth in him should not perish, but have everlasting life.***"

And that love that God has for us, is the greatest love anyone can ever have.

8   Conclusion

So you've looked (and I've written) a lot about what marriage is. We looked at the steps needed before you get married and the steps needed to stay married. There is a lot more involved in marriage than just putting on a tuxedo or dress and saying the words, "I do."

You need to do the "I do" part of marriage and live out what is required and desires of you when you make that vow before God and your spouse.

Marriage is a very special and wonderful event. It is an event that lasts a lifetime. Not everyone gets married, so if you are married, make sure you honor your marriage so that you can enjoy it until death parts you.

Salvation plan

Speaking of death, that is something that no one can avoid, so do you know where you will go for eternity once you die?

When you die, you are either going to go to Heaven or hell for ever and ever.

The only way to know for sure that you are going to Heaven is if you accept Jesus Christ into your heart to save you.

First, you have to know that you are a sinner, as stated in:

Romans 3:23: "*For all have sinned, and come short of the glory of God;*"

Second, you have to know that you deserve to go to hell for your sins, as also stated in:

Romans 6:23: "*For the wages of sin is death; but the gift of God is eternal life through Jesus Christ our Lord.*"

Third, Jesus Christ paid for your sins by dying on the cross (and then rising from the dead three days later), which you'll find in:

Romans 5:8: "*But God commendeth his love toward us, in that, while we were yet sinners, Christ died for us.*"

Fourth, if you confess and repent of your sins and believe that Jesus Christ is your savior and the only way to get to Heaven, you will be saved, as written in:

Romans 10:9-10: "*That if thou shalt confess with thy mouth the Lord Jesus, and shalt believe in thine heart that God hath raised him from the dead, thou shalt be saved. ¹⁰For with the heart man believeth unto righteousness; and with the mouth confession is made unto salvation.*" and see Romans 10:13: "*For whosoever shall call upon the name of the Lord shall be saved.*"

So if you believe all of this and are ready to be saved, say this prayer (the words do not have to be exact, as long as you mean the same thing):

Dear Lord, I know that I am a sinner that deserves to go to hell forever, but I also know that you came down to earth and lived a perfect life so that you can be the ultimate sacrifice by dying on the cross for my sins. I know that you rose again the third day, and the only way to get to Heaven is by believing in you. Lord, please forgive me of all my sins. Please come into my heart and save me from hell so that I can spend eternity with you in Heaven. Thank you so much for my salvation now and for everything you do for me. In Jesus name I pray, amen.

I told you I would include the salvation plan here, so please do not rush through this last part. If you need to, go back and read it again. If you still have questions about salvation, please consult a pastor or someone you know who can help you with this.

Thank you so much for your attention to this book. I pray that everyone who reads this book will be saved and have a successful and happy marriage.

God bless!

Acknowledgment

First, I thank my Lord and Savior, Jesus Christ, for everything He has done for me. Without Him, I would not have had the ability or the ambition to write this book. Second, I thank my wife for being the inspiration for this book and for supporting me to write a Christian marriage book. Kristen, I love that God brought us together, and I thank God daily for our wonderful marriage. And I also thank my children for giving me the immeasurable joy that fatherhood has given me through our marriage.

Throughout this book, I make references to the Bible. I use the King James Version (KJV) Bible. There are many versions of the Bible out there, and you can follow along with the Bible that you have. I use the KJV Bible because I have found through studies that it is the closest to the original language as we can have. It was translated directly from the original languages to English. Some other versions are a translation of a translation, which might have the tendency of losing meaning. I would never want to lose out on any meaning or message from God's Word. Some people say that the KJV is difficult to understand due to the "old time words." I understand that sometimes the Bible needs to be studied to understand it, but I am not a fan of changing any words in the Bible. The reason why literary scholars do not translate William Shakespeare is because they do not want anything to get lost in translation. Shakespeare is difficult to understand, and that is why they offer classes to study the original. The Bible covers this topic of not changing words or meaning in the Bible in Deuteronomy 4:2, Deuteronomy 12:32, and Revelation 22:18-19. I understand that we can not all learn the original languages of the Bible, so translations into the reader's language is necessary; but the Bible warns of how meaning can be lost when continuing to translate a translation.

ABOUT KHARIS PUBLISHING

KHARIS PUBLISHING is an independent, traditional publishing house with a core mission to publish impactful books, and channel proceeds into establishing mini-libraries or resource centers for orphanages in developing countries, so these kids will learn to read, dream, and grow. Every time you purchase a book from Kharis Publishing or partner as an author, you are helping give these kids an amazing opportunity to read, dream, and grow. Kharis Publishing is an imprint of Kharis Media LLC. Learn more at
  https://www.kharispublishing.com.

www.ingramcontent.com/pod-product-compliance
Lightning Source LLC
LaVergne TN
LVHW051604080426
835510LV00020B/3124